Free Verse Editions
Edited by Jon Thompson

STRANGE ANTLERS

Richard Jarrette

Parlor Press
Anderson, South Carolina
www.parlorpress.com

Parlor Press LLC, Anderson, South Carolina, 29621

Library of Congress Cataloging-in-Publication Data

Names: Jarrette, Richard, author.
Title: Strange antlers / Richard Jarrette.
Description: Anderson, South Carolina : Parlor Press, [2022] | Series: Free
  verse editions | Summary: "Strange Antlers is an homage to wisdom
  poets Sappho to Jane Hirshfield, particularly the Classical Chinese
  masters, whose verse comments are woven into the text as if in real time
  conversation on a mapless journey of healing from infancy to death and
  beyond"-- Provided by publisher.
Identifiers: LCCN 2021039418 (print) | LCCN 2021039419 (ebook) |
  ISBN
  9781643172798 (paperback) | ISBN 9781643172804 (pdf) | ISBN
  9781643172811 (epub)
Subjects: LCGFT: Poetry.
Classification: LCC PS3610.A773 S77 2022 (print) | LCC PS3610.A773
  (ebook) | DDC 811/.6--dc23
LC record available at https://lccn.loc.gov/2021039418
LC ebook record available at https://lccn.loc.gov/2021039419

978-1-64317-279-8 (paperback)
978-1-64317-280-4 (pdf)
978-1-64317-281-1 (ePub)

1 2 3 4 5

Cover art @ 2021 by Mark Russell Jones. Used by permission.
  https://www.markrusselljones.com/.
Cover design by David Blakesley.

Parlor Press, LLC is an independent publisher of scholarly and trade titles
in print and multimedia formats. This book is available in paperback and
ebook formats from Parlor Press on the World Wide Web at http://www.
parlorpress.com or through online and brick-and-mortar bookstores. For
submission information or to find out about Parlor Press publications, write
to Parlor Press, 3015 Brackenberry Drive, Anderson, South Carolina, 29621,
or email editor@parlorpress.com.

To the teachers

Contents

Contents

Contents

Strange Antlers

Assassins haunt

                            as smoke through trees
            blood whisper
                                        seasons
    owl.

The stag snakebit left hind leg may grow a deformed
rack right side of his head—strange antlers.

Unmoved by gods and heroes stars don't know their names
offer no history for my violent mythos—lucent

before the first prayer and after *the valley of the shadow
of death* and the unfinished evermore.

I trust myself to this lone paddle mused Wang Wei
afire on his deep page of moonlight.

A Dog's Skull Whistles

a dragon fly came to me
with news from my home
I lie in the afternoon
looking toward the hills

     —Jaime de Angulo

Crawling from Home in My Diaper at Ten Months Found on a Street in Los Angeles by a Truck Driver Who Began Knocking on Doors

A living weathercock crow studies the crossroads—
people heading in directions laid out for them.

Magnolia blossoms show the sky what they've made of root waters.

Mourning doves sparrows at their business wheeling
hawks and vultures test the borders of heaven.

I've been on the way to this flowering acacia all my life
hanging on to the reins of a cabbage butterfly.

Memory and the Paradoxes of Time as Wildfires Make Pyrocumulus Clouds

Some years seem to be searching
raise an eyebrow in my direction—message

from youth or pre-human ancestor
or Stephen Hawking's favorite unknown

—One mile north of the North Pole

asking a lot of the ears
as in soothing the tongues of silence

out of many-tongued starlight
versus dark matter.

Born confused by *here* versus *there*
known versus *unknown*
and by *versus*

say—all the years gathered and present
say—bushy tailed anteaters dust the bottom of the sea

father tender or violent without tells
pumping iron with the muscly swains or sisters
a mother's soft queries impaled.

Years wear ashes on their heads
like the crows and the fox sparrows.

After Fifty Years Return to the Beans in Kenneth Rexroth's Translation of Ou Yang Hsiu's *Jade Plum Trees in Spring* and Write This Poem with the Quill of a Swan

Beans a simile for the ripe green jade plums poem
savoring lazy hot afternoon sex a thousand years ago

the eyes of the figurehead of my heart the Black
Madonna strayed from those fragrant lowland fields

when my teacher from the mountains said

   —Yes, Mother Nature is beautiful when a swan
     trapped by ice in the frozen pond is eaten alive
     by the mother fox—terribly beautiful—
     and it is never finished.

Horses whinny by the river and a dog's skull whistles.

105 Degrees Already This Morning Startled by a Phainopepla Never Seen This Far North Wondering Why I'm Still Alive

Boy reads by refinery flare stack light
taste of sulphur on condemned air.

Owl glides into skew-jawed barn
lit dust to shadows one bird
or countless the reach of a life.

Eight years old a ground nest in Cats Forest—
slid out of a window to sleep there
no one knew no one to tell

something like an emperor penguin
guarding the egg on his feet.

Old Friends Say They Would Stop and Visit but the Appointment the Heat the Wife

You've got a shoe in the land of the dead and you're ghosting
invitations none these years friends uplifted fade away.

And what do you do when you want nothing from this human world?
Undertones of desire in the dear asking a murmuration of sorrows.

Assassin X skinned the dog and slipped the chain from its neck
—*I look forward with genuine pleasure to your future suffering.*

No matter the season winter lamentations—a mantle of work
toward the stilling of the phantom-weighing scales.

My Father Taught Me Many Strange Things
with Unexpected Consequences

I have been cut with a knife and I have cut with a knife.
My father gave me his combat steel at nine

—It's always loaded and never jams.

Later the blade sheathed and I said to a woman that her cutting
wounds might be hieroglyphs—a history—read the scars

with fingertips and she saying—*I can't bear to*
worlds of sand and thorn in our eyes.

Wordless Sudden Awakening Upon Finding William Merwin's Poem *Little Horse*

I hope you will come with me to where I stand
often sleeping and waking
by the patient water
that has no father nor mother

The fingers stopped
digging into my palms and unfurled

feelings seeing somewhere beyond seeing
through the deaths no language for

no more aware than a blade of grass
sunlight touches the tip of and it reaches.

At ten years fistfighting the boys
in my path hiding nights in the forest

something found in *Grapes of Wrath*
and I taught a few the word

shitheels but never told them
about *Rose of Sharon.*

After I Found My Father's Body at Home Edmund Kara Gave Me Lessons in Theology While Carving *The Phoenix* for the Nepenthe Terrace in Big Sur

The sculptor said he's about hair and waves of cloth
suffered a shock-mute boy drifting near who at last said

—*The unfinished hand*

of the outreaching left arm of Moses

—*will be a damning fist*

right holding tablets the Ten Commandments.

—*No a blessing palm*

turned to the Phoenix with mallet and chisel to bite
into ancient water cells inside her burl spitting at him

—*She's mocking me.*

Captured and Forced to Attend School I Went Silent a Special Ed Boy Gave Me a Treatise on *The Ten Ox Herding Pictures* and Said *You Should Have This*

Delighting under a ribbon of cliff shore waterfall
sleek as a sea hound on his rock in the seething
tides my fugitive home forever.

Seventy years toward mercy nation a ruin sharp
mother ninety-six yet applauds the malignant
regime we say *god* say *hot day* say *corn*

failing crow grasps steel rain gutter claws nicking.
Grim as wolf I attend to the mother on injured
roads twisted like ox guts.

Unleashed by Su Dong-Po's Confession

I allow myself to go a little wild
for one hundred years let me get drunk
thirty-six thousand times

The people I don't want to see things I don't want to do
became the entire world—roof gutter crow fall sage unhinged
parent giving the look between insolent and dead.

Are you touching the one I wish to avoid west wind
inflaming war and prayer flags? Later it was said neglect was also
the crime but nothing was happening I could tend my Cats

Forest nest swim a mile into the Pacific until houses and people
far off and pitiful—adrift in light and ancient songs of the sea.
Veils of steel gray rain dress the islands.

Idling on the Porch with Tu Fu Pondering and the Lorca Translations by Sarah Arvio

Tu Fu asks

—*How many times in one man's life*
  can he listen to heaven's music?

Neither sad nor happy the moon
makes its simple journey—

the bright stars and planets
it all seems like a gesture to keep up.

I won't be late.

Then come dreams of forgetting
taking the fall
enemies—

morning
yellow and black oriole in the pink myrtle
and bees.

Evils of the world draw their rasps

—*Wind shapes the dust*
  into silver prows

In These Twisted and Perilous Times
Having Barbaric Thoughts I Confer with
Po Chü-i and His Elder Tu Fu

More cockeyed looks from crows and sparrows anthrax bearing
carcasses rise from ice and tundra—nation an egg in midair
tossed by the vicious thug who relishes suffering
cheered by his minions.

    —There's drought south of the Yangste: in Ch'ü-chou
      people are eating people says Po Chü-i.

The president locks brown babies in cages—
I want to tear his eyes out and crush his trachea.

    —They sacrificed a beautiful white stallion
      and swore their oath in its blood says Tu Fu.

Laughter in winter as seasonal creeks awakened to flood
roads we splashed across broke ice in the fountain each morning
for birds spring black violets cracked through rocks to feed
the larvae of giant leopard moths my first pets.

The Black Madonna of Częstochowa bleeds in my fist.

From the Memory of a Kind Word the Touch of a Friend's Hand with Lines of Tu Fu and Conversation with Charles Simic

The vault of heaven falls in—
mourning and reaching with Tu Fu
I set a weary heart to rest under the linden

*—All things caught between shield and sword
    all grief empty the clear night passes.*

Shall you inherit the earth little sparrow
Job's vineyard flourish again?
One instant of love glint of irrational hope

beginner throws his mayfly
into the Missouri River and draws out
a leviathan into merciful hands.

One-eyed Satan blinks.

Charles Simic said his grandmother held his little
hand picking their way through bombed
Belgrade going to the movies

*—Wizard of Oz
    but SS officer smiling at us a few chairs away
    not such a good thing.*

—What do you think of our current situation?

*—Oh ho what a question.
    We've learned nothing—the same vile ideas
    and vile practices keep returning—
    nostalgia for concentration camps
    and slavery for other people of course.*

—I cling to what peace one twig holds

murmurs Tu Fu.

Wind Annoys Frankie the Kitten He Takes My Knees to Reboot the Whiskers Refuge a Plain of Sudden War

Su Dong-Po's been listening nine hundred years
—*I know that each year grief*
  shall twist your innards.

News from the Capitol worse than imagined
the junta bibled in another rapist
shifty butcher's thumb

weight for mephitic schemes.
The Black Madonna of Częstochowa
weeps from the Tartar arrow throat wound

Hussite saber cuts into her cheek medallion
heavier than the serpentine rock
of Figueroa Mountain

the pines and the cinnamon colored bear. Falcons
read the gyres blue riven by Vandenberg
Air Force Base bombers.

A Rage Too Complicated Sought Mei Yao-Ch'en
Hoping to Pick through *the artless simplicity of
his mind* to Find *the profound spiritual insight he's
known for* and Imagined What He Might Say

He's annoyed with the shit-
maggot stuffed crows

in his treetops crying
omens to the west wind.

Calls me a broken leg
goose a sitting duck says

—*It's one thing to bury weapons
under the pigs another to savor
white garlic pan fried in dew.
It's just a tired horse with a nose
for home after the wars.*

I Turn to Grandmother's Things for Succor

William Merwin said

—On the last day of the world
  I would want to plant a tree

leaves brushing clouds roots
touching deep waters the dead.

—And what would you do he asked.

—Plant grandmother I said
  mother's mother

though the youngest touching
her casket said

—She's with the smooth god.

I keep her things
by the bed—#12 thimble

ibis scissors
bone crochet hooks

from before the war
the Civil War—

when taken by the dark hours
I touch them.

Unfurling the Rivers and Mountains Scroll
of a Life Taking Stock for the Children

So many steps into confusion utter clarity seems familiar.
I must be getting somewhere.

August heroes fall twenty by twenty—
fell on my sword for one misplaced heroic ideal after another.

The dime I turned on
eye to eye with a jaguar—jaw like a Mack truck

grave as Abraham Lincoln
mind plain to read

—*I know how much you are I know if you kiss dogs.*

To the Woman Who Made a Wide Detour to Avoid Me Just the Two of Us Walking on Pfeiffer Beach Big Sur

Clouds opened one blue eye gazing at a lake of light
on the charcoal gray sea

goldeneyes struggle through waves
that carved the headlands.

Years later I realized the ducks were feeding in the turmoil
of Aleutian storms reaching twenty-four hundred miles southeast.

Not hard to imagine why you would avoid a lone man
so far off the highway in winter.

On the Photograph of a Man Laughing in North Carolina and Not Knowing Him

I blunder into spider webs turn my ankles in potholes
nothing like T'ao Ch'ien *lingering a moon out to the end.*

My father Roy—run off at seventeen by his father landing blows
all the way to the end of the dirt lane with a baseball bat—

seemed happy only in mountains he knew hollows to ridgelines
old waters left me years there with sister aunts and his mother

who loved the singing of Doc Watson down near in Deep Gap.
My friend recalls that soon after we crossed the state line

on our way to find the graves and some livermush and ramps
the man at the wheel strangled a laugh under an iron bridge.

When I Steered My Father Through
the Tasseling Corn

Roy Estone's dark wings were made of biblical knives
timeworn as the shawl of Moses—

brushed my face last night like the black moth
that shares his weakness for honey.

An elder woman seized my wrist at his brother's funeral

—I'm going to give you the Word.
I loved your father
everyone loved your father
black brown red white old young man woman child
and he loved everybody.

He still carries me on his shoulders at times
through the tasseling corn

above the copperheads and rattlers
as I navigate toward Uncle John's store—

the skew-jawed shack where he sold tobacco and sugar
and said *Hey* and I said *Hey* back

—Hot day-Hot day
Hot tomorrow-Hot tomorrow
Corn tasseling-Corn tasseling

and gave me a hunk of wild Grandfather Mountain
honeycomb he'd set aside in a jar under

the counter with the corn whiskey that made Aunt
Ruby's teeth gleam through her red lipstick.

On Wang Wei's Lines

Appearance emerges from chance conditions
and our true nature's empty kindred to nothing

Running around in a man for seventy years
dulling the blade on ghost assassins

               resolute acceptance of death

drinking the wake of Mater Dolorosa
from clouds on Pear Lake above the sequoia

drowsy timber rattler
orchard snow of wild-flying apple blossoms

              this whole empty skin drifting.

My son says you're not the only man who knows
pain—rung—the funeral bell in rain.

Clouds Mixed with the Smoke of Another Fifty Homes Burning in Fires South of Here

Mosquitos fed at my body last night
carry a taste of its pulse on the air.

Ravaged long ago a heart can still give
a little and just beyond the light sorrow.

Intending to Discharge Rage from Primal Injury Yet Taken by Its Futile Logic

Hot winds scourge bobcats and horses reset borders of wildfire
territories in a moment too late not wanting this to find me

rat in the rattler's throat jackrabbit flying. The kitten has a fine
intelligent gaze knows I'm too much to eat lap safe

from desperate coyotes feeding on house pets. Nervous deer
close on the town flagpole last night entire world condemned

by Nebuchadnezzar my rage growls in dead languages bristles
knives and battle spears generations honed—subito violence

of an outcast father seething queens in grandmother's obedience—
war blade lashed to the mangled hand waving off flies.

Mad Thug President Seeks to Roll Back Clean
Emission Rules Against Industry Advice as
War Against Violent Thoughts Lurches on

A yellow-rumped warbler locks eyes
with the transfixed cats

who confer nose to nose
settling on a cool path stone.

The sun takes its startling heat over rooftops
and the withered western ridge.

Falling into a Metaphysical Abyss I Visit
Tu Fu for Guidance After the Catastrophic
An Lu-Shan Rebellion Near the End of His Life

I follow the Master's chant to his house

—Don't condemn heroes to weep like heavy rains leave
  men to grain women to silk let us go in song again.

I'm in torment—my country ruled by enemies
millions of soldiers once defeated

violent mobs cheer some low imposter
as he destroys their farms banishes patriots.

Tu Fu weeps for his nation
dead son and daughter

wracked by malarial fevers
yet smiles through the bone piercing drizzle

offers what's left of the good floating-ant wine.
Sing an old song with me he says

—Just now as we meet again the season of falling
  blossoms gracing the world how lovely it is.

Apart from Righteous Fury at the Neo-Nazis
Maybe Some of This Rage Is Aging Melancholy

The ten swords in my spine clashing crown to tailbone

severed my wings
cat's cradles my nerves
slaked never—

puzzle for King Arthur
the Black Madonna
Solomon

or Sappho
or Smokey the Cat
whose tail trembles when I stroke her spine.

I'm just the man with a stiff back and a limp singing Elvis
Presley to a picture of Mary Brown

who died when we were eleven.
What fingers will find the strings of my harp?

I Seek Direction from Red Pine
Quechua Midwives and Li Po

Clouds seem newborn moment to moment from the blue
forehead of the sky an imagination
larger than imagination.

Red Pine says

—Nothing could be deeper than the womb
of the Goddess of Transcendent Wisdom.

Is that how you throw a saddle over a cloud?
Quechua midwives of the Ecuadorian Amazon say

—Death has no schedule
takes elders and the young
so we teach as many as we can.

In high summer meadow crickets uplift desire—
un concours de chant—to the seven visible planets

—The eye reaches beyond what ruins our lives

says Li Po.

With Po Chü-i in Early September

Everything scatters away—everything

The territory I've settled might seem narrow yet
one cabbage butterfly portal to the Swan—

four blocks the café journey gospels of chair and footstool
rock among sage flowers bees at business black-chinned

hummingbirds overfeeding for the migration to central Mexico.
Once renting a block south eye level to a gray squirrel's

tree other side of second floor blinds
she traveled the same black wires rats run at twilight

chattered from the café pine—*What the hell you doing here?*
She won't scold the forgotten moved a mile west.

Do you remember the across the road birch sky?
Its winter was great grandmother Mary's hair so who forgave

the like scribbles in her childhood McGuffey's Reader
my first lines there obscuring the lessons.

A Fifty Dollar Bill Flutters Out Of A Book I Think Has The Poem In It I'm Looking for and Letters from William Stafford Robert Aitken and Ram Dass

I took the monk-vow of poetry—unknown
and not a steel penny.

Sappho thrums

—But all is to be dared
              because even a person of poverty . . .

Five people seem to enjoy this company a scrub jay
perches on the patio chair afternoons

baristas often kind.

Dragonflies lit on the boy's shoulders that time
he sunned himself on a rock in the creek.

Ram Dass says
—If you see a particularly
  contemplative one say hello.

Don't drink much anymore no painkiller
wash my face in crows trade a book for a cup of wine
everything for the greening kiss.

Stafford says
—I'll try all the harder.

Grandmotherly Aitken teaches
—Do you have a teacher?

Admiring Ridgelines above the Valley
Remembering My Blue Ridge Grandmother
Hessie Mae Poteet's Cautions to Be Careful in
the Woods Because a Big Black Racer Snake
Would Wrap Around Me and I'd Never
Get It Off Even If I Was to Roll All the Way Down
Grandfather Mountain to the North Fork River

Upland jays at labors
fox and bear on the mountain

volant raptors gyre
golden squirrel and rat aware.

O summer's beauty
southern pacific rattlesnake

how glad not to step
on your crawling

cuzzo.

Not Wanting This Autumn Poem but the River —
Again the Death House of Huck's Pap and Mine

Kindred hearts lament

—*Mercy*
the heated women who desire
President Bone Saw . . .

Ravening cruelty
severed single wings
beat the ground—

crazy thoughts
root memories slip by the *firesnakes*
tangle with the silent boy's
mother blood knot.

The sober psychiatrist offered a more
fitting name misunderstood
Grendel said

—*It's interesting to think*
of your mother in terms of the men
that she's loved.

The coroner pondered knife and screwdrivers
I'd driven into my father's skull
during our death battle
in the dream said

—*What beautiful patterns*
you made inside his brain.

The father my father's knife gave to me.

At Times Brutal and Violent Filled with Sexual Swagger My Father Nevertheless Handed Down Knowledge of Healing Powers in the Wild

Faint bell tones rise from the river valley
against descending breezes off the mountains

old wounds drawn into their brushing by
fanned by goshawks and white-eyed vireos.

Yang Wan-Li's Line and the Possible

Suddenly he's a lone goose balanced on a bent reed

A crow beak-roots in the flowers bees express sincere
interest in my right ear maybe the tinnitus so loud

believe that's a lush summer meadow in there singing.
I'd row out on a lake of melancholy but hear my daughter's

concerns about that melon collie howling in the graveyard
and why it made Huck and Tom so nervous.

Demons drilling like the devil in my spine clock out

the jay could find an emerald ring

I could be purged with hyssop.

Of W.S. Merwin's *Elegy for a Walnut Tree*
Against Morbid and Violent Fantasies

and all these years I have looked through your limbs
to the river below and the roofs and the night
and you were the way I saw the world

Little black and yellow
little butterfly
you make the dying juniper pretty—

cabbage white
you take my life for a wild ride
flashing it back so fast—

through your pink flowers myrtle
a buzzard takes my spleen
into the clouds.

If This the Last Thing I Say

Hot ground airs
stir white oleander

hidden in core shadows
the upland jay asks.

Becalmed pines will not rock
the nested owls

late afternoon arrives
pierced by green hummingbirds.

How can I say *recluse?*

I have broken
and have been broken

bedeviled nights
I seek out the Swan.

Toward a Hidden River with No Human Name

a little bit toward evening I saw him
who was searching
I followed him into the shadows step by step
and all of a sudden he vanished

—Jaime de Angulo

Pondering Flight of the Milky Way 2.2 Million Km an Hour Toward the Shapley Concentration Looking for Han Shan in the Wines of Spain

Han Shan must have known with forest and streams
hermitage cave and the hearts of dogs flying

—People take the Cold Mountain way never arrive.

Maestro Tempranillo stirs

—Should've been here an hour ago I'm gone.
   Should've been here an hour ago Grass Mountain Gone.
   Should've been here an hour ago you're gone.

Horned owls on the wind moonlit chaos
notes of cedar and riverine valley in the mouth

—A blind man who shoots for a sparrow's eye just might score a hit.

Maybe my fontanel had the way and I reach
for where it was and remember.

Startled by the Mind in Merwin's Couplet

what we see again will come to us in secret
and without even knowing that we are here

A bronze afternoon again the lit window in his absence
slant of the sun he recalls and welcomes to glance

at his ashes then
purling with the shimmering river

in and out of the shadows of willows
on his way to the sea

sunlight through the jeweled flowing
stippling the backs of fishes and the old mother rock

The Black Madonna and a Crow's Wake

Kissed Our Lady of Częstochowa carried my heart
into a day that was one guttering candle in a cathedral

not thinking stopped under the ancient blue oak eyes
drawn to some sixty crows among branches

fence neighbor's abandoned shed roof all of them still
then to the eye at my feet overspilling absence of a crow—

our drinking the journey in sobered the landscape
elder brother gone ahead certain we were already there.

Death and Resurrection in Meng Chiao's
murderous furnace at the heart of change
in His Poem *Laments for the Gorges*

what of that thirst for wisdom when you're
suddenly here, dead center in these waters?

I forgave a priest sermons for the comfort of communion
—*The Body of Christ the bread of heaven*
—*The Blood of Christ the cup of salvation*

wisecracked
—*If no crucifixion no resurrection.*

Meng Chiao catalogued gruesome deaths offered by the perilous
Triple Gorges to travelers fisherman immortal poets anyone—

a democracy of Death the *giveaway* of Death—this
devouring the resurrection this dying the big aria

dragons applauding with their lips again.

On Wang Wei's *Farewell to Yang*
Who's Leaving for Kuo-chou

Those canyons are too narrow to travel
how will you make your way there . . .

I'm a duck walking ten thousand miles
listening hard to my hair

Jane Hirshfield's peeled hedgehogs
my fellows because

you've got to mind your steps
and about this mile marker—

the wily old monk left his begging sign
—*Only obstacle to the path the path*

Of Su Tung-p'o's Comment on His Friend

He's simply an echo of mountaintop moonlight
coming and going night after night

Sycamore thrashes
two-trunk pine sways

unclean spirits in human form burn the world
sparrows and jays forage in the manzanita—

we attend to the ballet of the firmament
wild church psalter brittle leaf

telling of green palaces
the vanished waters.

Cutthroats Assassinate the Sky As They Did the Sweet Federico Whose Threat Was the Legacy of Silverio Franconetti

To a wronged and musk-scented woman

—*When you shoot your dark*
  eyes into the night Orion's dogs die.

It was satisfying to say such things
and we bit deeper into the marrow of the hidden.

The meadow animal with heat and cicadas
in the prickly fiddlenecks she said

—*The sky is a river of songs and I hear sometimes*
  the siguiriya of Lorca's Franconetti

and she knew the lines

—*His cry was formidable*
  the old folks say
  that their hair stood on end
  and that the mirrors
  spilled mercury

Wind tore the shroud of wildfire smoke
spilling the deeps we'd tasted

pulsing in the wound
Death placed on Silverio's soul

in the forges of the cantaores
who settled things with their knives

where teachers attacked the limits
and the limits cowered when he released

the beheaded Dionysian scream.

Asked in a Dream for a Poem About the Master Who Died We Sit in a Dreamworld of the Dead

—You're not so far away after.
—Neither are you.

We're idling on the banks of the Santa Inés
of landscape we sit in deep communion
Li Po and Wang Wei sail by singing.

Drifting awake
a whisper reaches for my renowned
old teacher by the river

—It would be like my favorite cat
*   killing and eating my favorite bird*

but the cleverness makes me heartsick

—A dust mote of lit joy at the bottom of the sea.

In Red Pine's Commentary on the Heart Sutra and the Line *form is emptiness emptiness is form* He Cites Edward Conze and I Decide to Hold It Like an Avocado Seed in a Poem

The infinitely Far-away is not only near but infinitely near.
It is nowhere, and nowhere it is not. This is the mystical
identity of opposites. Nirvana is the same as the world.
It is not only 'in' and 'with you'—you are nothing but it.

Gary Snyder says

—*It will just squirt away like an avocado seed*
  if you try to squeeze it.

A scrub jay considers from the green-black shadows
weird sound licks my nape tears the wolf around
to meet the gang of assassins—

feral instinct lofty thought left wing right wing of the high
soaring buzzard sailing northeast with clouds
over the Chumash painted caves.

Chef Aota says

—*All my chi goes into the pot.*

Li Po Scolded by Blossoms You Let Your Grief Go Then I Found It Which Drowned an Old Demon

Not gibbons from both banks of your river as you sailed toward Tu Fu
but crows cracking wise or starving or fuck off

to the unfeathered clod by the gone river willows
twelve months a year dead dog bone dry—

clung to your book memorized the breezes studied poems
about you slipped my soul into your grief-laden reach

for the edge of heaven—war blade heavier than the boat taken by sand
where the long bright tongue of moonlight my river was.

Jane Hirshfield's Comment During an Interview
about Her Poem *In a Kitchen Where Mushrooms Were
Washed* and on the Source of Her Poems from a Letter

A crow grooms his mate in a pool of morning light
Jane's voice rising from the pink crepe myrtle

—Much to my surprise I knew the joy of the truffle pig
and I'm preening pig feathers in the Kingdom Of Heaven.

In Jane's letter she said
—Jack Gilbert and you work hard at writing

but doesn't think of herself as a writer
—Poems just seem to come like mushrooms in the night.

O to be both pig and its joy food.

Cry4 mRNA

The cabbage butterfly enters house left wild exits house right
wild toils north above the stone path toward St. Mark's.

I don't know what it knows about its way.

Bird eye proteins perceive wave lengths of blue light
required to see magnetic fields all becoming migration flyways

aligned in quantum coherence—baby knees and palms pulled
my feet and diaper into Los Angeles traffic this far.

Simple Poem with Roy Orbison

People plant a lot of rosemary and thyme.
When I have a chicken to cook

I walk down the street and pick twigs.
Sunlight came a long way to make the plants beautiful.

From the beginning
it was a long road for the chicken and me.

I don't know where we're going
but it's together

with the dust of Genghis Khan and the gold dust
of his hoard on the cosmic wind.

I was once sent up ahead
on the high notes of Roy Orbison.

At a Confluence of Conze Porete Hirshfield and Po Chü-i

Edward—*Nirvana, the infinitely Far-away is infinitely near*
Marguerite—*God, the FarNear, His Farness is the more Near*
Jane—*To be that porous, to have such largeness pass through me*

Windblown pine bough reverie uplifted in Po Chü-i's large grasp
—Magisterial rock windswept and pure bamboo so lavish
   and green they seem full of sincerity

deepened by memory of the overlooked cinnamon black bear sow
groaning to her feet *infinitely near* the moment we stood to gather
picnic empty bottles of pinot gris cab franc twilight—*Egyptian*

violet more intense than the phthalos we'd crowed—freeze-framed
reading hindquarters of beast shambling through fiddlenecks toward
FarNear Coulter Pines—*To be that porous, to have such largeness . . .*

Neither Heaven Nor Earth Far at Times

Dogs howl at sirens of first responders
racing toward the broken people.

I've lived five sides of this equation
equal to the riddle of life.

The fine trembling of the scales
begins to calm near autumn equinox

a chance approaches to be carried
in the before the beginning

the after the end. Little sparrow—
dear mortal heart—will you be sipping

the horizon with the legion of Mongolian
swans lifting at midnight?

Li Po Answers My Question about Shame with Praise for His Friend the Musician

I swear by the warm belly of that truck driver
who found a baby in the street and cradled him

evermore sought the mother in wombs
like Huck Finn's sugar hogshead Jackson's

Island ground nest in Cats Forest longings
a susurrus in the trees the night sky.

Is there some mastery that deserves
love horizon stop and wait for me?

—*When he plays even in a first few notes*
  I hear the pines of ten thousand valleys.

I know the rage of a dog at the end of his chain
but for a moment once was looking back

from the other side of the river in a horse.

I Grasp the Horns of the Sublime

Laurel branch nods with the weight of mockingbird
rufous-sided towhees forage in the white sage.

All heeds as the sun drops below withered uplands
night tails hawk fall scrapes the eaves of St. Mark's.

No word from the children traveling to a funeral
one late vireo dives into the firethorn.

Seasons above and Below

Exhausted peach tree talks
with dry wind and the occasional

bird of things I see and things
I cannot see in the unlit worlds

and last night's news of the Swan
close moon everywhere

missed serious conversation
sparrows explain in their cockeyes.

In the Economy of Nature Hearing Joy Harjo

We were all given gifts to share, even the animals,
even the plants, minerals, clouds—all beings

A crow breaks from her flock at gleaning to read
the face under a hat they know as the puzzle.

Perhaps they'd painted corvid voodoo on its mind
to open the *giveaway hand* these crow years.

Learning That Ticks Are Born with Six Legs and Grow Two More After Feeding on Blood I Composed This Taxonomy of a Prayer

Thus Shariputra without attainment
bodhisattvas take refuge in Prajnaparamita
and live without walls of the mind

White-throated sparrows at forage soul at matins.
Aunt Maxine and I pulled ticks off feral cats she'd half tamed

in the forest off each other in secret. I've been the tick
holding on for delicious ideas to near teachers

to feed my way into carried far—*thrilling*—to see my host
vanish through walls I can't scale on fifty-six knees.

Captured by W.S. Merwin's Poem
Still and Its Last Line

while the seamless water slipped past under the reflections

Beyond the borders of France
hoofprints of dear Coquette the Donkey
trail from your words and off the page

—Gone gone to the other shore already there fully awake.

Heat draws sap from the pine one
drip snaps the crown of an old Borsalino
with the hollow sound of an empty pail.

Assassination School and Your Wise
Blood Question So Young Federico

Trees
have your rough roots found
my heart in the dirt

Maybe there is a tree near Granada returning your green to the stars
or a frail lamppost in a blind alley and your shivering

Egyptian violet shadow

because the Chair of Death assigned killers
grave robbers next to murder

honey and wounds.

I look for you in books and see the animal I met
in my daughter's face when they leapt into the dark lake

hear little brother who made the headdress when he was six

—I'm King of the Dogs the Monkeys and the Snakes.

The King palmed my Audubon birdcall and appeared at second
twilight out of his lair in the secret woods

—I called a train I called the wind
and I called down the stars

asked how old everything is where it's from
said I didn't know

gave him the meteorite I bought for five dollars
off the desert rockhound

—From somewhere older than earth is.

We beheld moonrise through black
wings of the pines Federico.

Dante and the Last Candle

Already the night could see all of the stars
of the other pole and ours was so low
it never rose above the ocean floor

My companion gutters in late twilight
Our Lady of Sorrows

steps out of the deep window
into her dominion.

Stars and dark matter
murmur—the lyre of Sappho aeterna . . .

Refuge in the Simple

Leaf stirs then branch pine needle then bough
arroyo cottonwoods light painting green

root tendrils reaching farther from the sun
toward a hidden river with no human name

Although Forbidden I Played a Few Chords on Chopin's Piano in Valldemossa Mallorca

Children
make that
the epitaph

Rumor of Your Passage as Starlight

if he tells you: I want nothing
let him go
straight to heaven

—Jaime de Angulo

i

Mockingbird's white wing bars flare in dense evergreen—
wild mastery in the corner of an eye shooting stars

behind a word of Meng Hao-jan—melt into a night in the day
of Coulter Pine return on the wings of the Swan.

ii

When lost I look to the sky—
I've been running into a burning factory kissing.

Death moves the white pieces with experience
three clouds the semiotics of *darkens*

wisdom once *an ear to the Great Below* in Sumer
river valley meadows become voiceless.

A pocket church of light opens in the turning quince
for a hummingbird that stills her wings.

iii

Storm shaken pine hurled nest recluse heart
not most *pure in*

threadbare

deceived as the one in ten violinist
in tune after killing nine.

Li Po's drink-to

*—Nothing left but a river flowing
    on the borders of heaven.*

Quanta of light live a quintillion years
just a blink to a photon it's said.

When I imagine lingering the all of it out
to the all of the way

    the Swan
           further
                  lux aeterna
        further
            imperishable communion
        further

far the reach of the where.

iv

Among vibrating star particles bearing my name

dewdrop
at the headwaters of time

ribbon of cliff shore
waterfall

the end

—icy and dark
  sleeping irises of my evil?

Lorca at twenty
the murder of Cambodia

at my twenty
among vibrating star particles bearing my name.

V

Master Musō looks up

—Crimes and errors
fill the whole sky
and who knows it

Blood-weary
I step out of the medieval armor
airs touching skin
from a land of clover honey?

Autumn sends its palette to the six directions—
I've been there and there besieged
illusions sought the wise

signed papers got something
gave something
like the people in their important silver cars.

I watch them
and what was written off
go.

Yes breeze
you don't attend to shame
but scars and the ruins
and hollows.

vi

I've seen billions of years beyond the Northern
Cross and I'm still swatting horse flies.

Captured daylong by a cloud Tu Mu says
—*It has no mind at all, no mind and surely no talent*

Tu's *and* larger than the stride
of my man's and and . . .

like our galaxy exiting its black hole into a newborn
universe and its own time

and its Noh theater crone
fluent in gestures of the gone.

From the untranslatable crawling away and toward.

vii

North wind shakes an acorn into my cup
tangles the living and dead

near heartbeats
spike at the scrub jay's question

spangled is
the earth with her crowns

Sappho thrums.

Seven winters of soughs from the grave
Ekaterina hushing

I am fragments
a fractal equation
each fragment an infinitude of fragments
you can't change this

The roof edge crow sips the seven seas
from his steel rain gutter.

viii

Running in unforeseen rain

Stop

a woman from the sea of memory opens her eyes to clouds—
you'd think I was alone.

On our face fall the vanished rivers.

Madrone and miner's lettuce leaves shine
slender oat stalks bow.

ix

The season tells in gossamer
whorl of chaff and whisper.

The crow selects a twig then
drops onto a man's hat

sparrows scratch by the shoes—
verse for tonight's death owl

high valley aspen the glittering
choir of spent Charon coins.

X

T'ao Ch'ien finds the whole try in ruins a thousand
years already it's toward the unnamed we drink.

Scaffolds around my mind collapse in a G major
cascade like the Goldberg Variations I love.

Scrapers and painters fly off to other jobs or perish
in the nothing I've paid them to make something of.

xi

A cabbage white crosses the road
straight on eye to eye

All right

until emptied of stories
like Buddhists buying animals in the marketplace

and turning them loose
the last one

xii

There's a feeling like walking on water
or along the tips of wet grass
without leaving footprints

nor breaking the spine of one green blade
believing that grass and water
will uplift to the sun

rumor of your passage as starlight
in the form of two feet and the barnyard
they set out from that morning

xiii

The southwest wind shimmers
sunlight on yellow leaves

a day so autumn pure it praises
the sorrow of countless farewells

xiv

One sparrow claw
nicks the mooring line free

wings of the Swan
belly the sails

the leer of my assassin
grows small

stars turn
I trust the pilot's eyes

and the wheel

Notes

Italicized words and lines not noted below are dialogue or monologue actual or imagined.

Preface

Line 7: *strange antlers*—technical name for antlers deformed by injury. Explains unicorns.

Lines 10–11: Psalm 23 *Bible*.

Line 12: *Mountain Home* David Hinton (2002) Wang Wei "Adrift on the Lake" pg 71.

First Chapter Epigraph

Home Among the Swinging Stars Jaime de Angulo (2006) "to A.J." pg 32.

Memory and the Paradoxes of Time

Line 5: Stephen Hawking interview—*What happened before the Big Bang? That's like asking what's* one mile north of the North Pole.

After Fifty Years Return to the Beans

One Hundred Poems from the Chinese Kenneth Rexroth (1971) pg 53.

Lines 6–9: Marie-Louise von Franz lecture.

Old Friends Say They Would Stop and Visit

Line 3: After Po Chü-i in Hinton (2002) "Off Hand Chant" pg 172.

Line 6: Personal communication *Assassin X* to author.

Wordless Sudden Awakening

Animae W. S. Merwin (Kayak, 1969) "Little Horse" pg 15.

After I Found My Father's Body at Home

Edmund Kara (1925–2001) Sculptor, Big Sur. "The Phoenix" yet presides at *Nepenthe*.

Captured and Forced to Attend School

"10 Bulls by Kakuan" in Reps & Sensaki *Zen Flesh, Zen Bones* (1958) pgs 165–187.

Line 9: After Ezra Pound *Poems and Translations* (2003) "Exiles Letter" by Rihaku (Li Po) *I won't say it / wasn't hard going, / Over roads twisted like sheeps' guts* pg 256.

Unleashed by Su Dong-Po's Confession

Dreaming of Fallen Blossoms: Tune Poems of Su Dong-Po Yun Wang (2019) "To the Tune of *The Court Fills with Fragrance*" pg 41.

Idling on the Porch with Tu Fu Pondering

Lines 2–3: *Crossing The Yellow River* Sam Hamill (2000) Tu Fu "Song for a Young General" pg 152.

Lines 16–17: *Poet In Spain—Federico García Lorca* Sarah Arvio (2017) "Bells for the Dead" pg 153. Arvio adheres to Lorca's unpunctuated manuscript originals.

In These Twisted and Perilous Times

Lines 5–6: *Classical Chinese Poetry* David Hinton (2008) Po Chü-i "Song Of Ch'in-Chou" pg 273.

Lines 9–10: Hamill (2000) Tu Fu "The Thatched Hut" pg 158.

From the Memory of a Kind Word

Lines 4–5: *The Selected Poems of Tu Fu* David Hinton (1989) "Restless Night" pg 69.

Lines 16–24: Conversation with Charles Simic, Brattleboro, Vermont 2017.

Line 25: Hinton (1989) Tu Fu "Overnight At Headquarters" pg 69.

Wind Annoys Frankie the Kitten

Lines 2–3: Wang (2019) Su Dong-Po "To the Tune of *From the River City*" pg 65.

A Rage Too Complicated Sought Mei Yao-Ch'en

Hinton (2008) from his introduction to Mei Yao-Ch'en and a collage from various poems pgs 338–350. Mei's counsel imagined.

I Turn To Grandmother's Things for Succor

Lines 2–3: *The Essential Merwin* W. S. Merwin (2017) "Place" pg 207.

On the Photograph of a Man Laughing

Line 2: Hinton (2002) T'ao Ch'ien "After Kuo Chu-pu's Poems" *I can / linger this exquisite moon out to the end* pg 10.

Line 10: Homage "Hobo Bridge" at the tracks—conclave that suffered a mad child of the fringes.

On Wang Wei's Lines

The Selected Poems of Wang Wei David Hinton (2006) "In the Mountains, for My Brothers" pg 57.

Line 3: *A Book of Five Rings* Miyamoto Musashi (1974) Victor Harris, Translator *the way of the warrior is a <u>resolute acceptance of death</u>* pg 38.

Line 8: After Tu Fu in Hinton (2002) "Inscribed On A Wall At Chan's Recluse Home" *bottomless dark, the way / here lost—I feel it drifting, this whole empty boat* pg 98.

Falling into a Metaphysical Abyss

Lines 2–3: Hinton (1989) Tu Fu "Song For Silkworms And Grain" pg 111.

Line 12: Hinton (1989) Tu Fu "Facing Snow" pg 110 *floating-ant wine* The good stuff after ant scum poured off. See Hinton's note pg 161.

Lines 14–15: Hinton (1989) Tu Fu "Meeting Li Kuei-Nien South Of The River" pg 111.

I Seek Direction from Red Pine

Lines 5–6: *The Heart Sutra* Red Pine (2004) pgs 50–51.

Line 13: *un concours de chant*—singing competition.

Line 14: *The Selected Poems of Li Po* David Hinton (1996) "On Hsin-P'ing Tower" pg 50.

With Po Chü-i in Early September

The Selected Poems of Po Chü-i David Hinton (1999) "To Get Over A Spring Heartfelt And Long, Written During The Seclusion Fast" pg 184.

Lines 12–13: Mary Bell Sawyer Ives (1866–1965)—her *McGuffey's Readers* I scribbled in.

A Fifty Dollar Bill Flutters out of a Book

Lines 4–5: *If not, Winter: Fragments of Sappho* Anne Carson (2002) "31" pg 63.

Lines 12–13: Personal communication Ram Dass.

Line 18: Personal communication William Stafford.

Line 20: Personal communication Robert Aitken Roshi.

Yang Wan-Li's Line and the Possible

Hinton (2002) "Crossing Open-Anew Lake" pg 266.

Line 8: *Bible* KJV Psalm 51:7 *Purge me with hyssop, and I shall be clean: wash me and I shall be whiter than snow.* I share an appreciation for the Psalm with Anne Carson—"Hyssop, it's like mint from outer space." Interview.

Of W.S. Merwin's *Elegy for a Walnut Tree*

The Moon Before Morning W. S. Merwin (2014) pg 62.

Second Chapter Epigraph

Jaime de Angulo (2006) "Other Song of the Shaman" pg 38.

Pondering Flight of the Milky Way

The Shapely Concentration—galactic supercluster drawing the Milky Way.

Line 3: Hinton (2008) Han Shan "304" pg 220.

Line 10: *The Collected Songs of Cold Mountain* Red Pine (2000) "113" pg 113.

Startled by the Mind in Merwin's Couplet

Merwin (2014) "Long Afternoon Light" pg 88.

Death and Resurrection

Hinton (2002) from "Forward" pg 142.

Meng Chiao quote from "(Lament) 9" pg 145.

Line 8: *Conflict Resolution For Holy Beings* Joy Harjo (2015) "For Calling The Spirit Back From Wandering The Earth In Its Human Feet" *Make a giveaway and remember, keep the speeches short* pg 6.

On Wang Wei's *Farewell to Yang*

The Selected Poems of Wang Wei Davi Hinton (2006) pg 89.

Line 3: *Given Sugar, Given Salt* Jane Hirshfield (2001) "The Poet Looks At Her Poems" *She looks at the pages: / now the world silent as beach stones, raw as <u>peeled hedgehogs</u>* pg 61.

Line 8: Barry Spacks reading from manuscript 2010 or so.

Of Su Tung-p'o's Comment on His Friend

Hinton (2002) "At Brahma-Heaven Monastery, Following the Rhymes in a Short Poem of Crystalline Beauty by the Monk Acumen-Hoard" pg 225

Cutthroats Assassinate the Sky

Lines 9 & 24: *Deep Song and Other Prose: Federico García Lorca* C. Maurer Editor-Translator (1975) "Play and Theory of the Duende" pgs 42–53. Silverio Franconetti (1831–1889) renowned cantaor—Diego el Fillo (1806–1854) his Romani teacher who worked the forges near Seville.

Lines 11–15 Arvio (2017) "Flamenco Vignettes" pg 159

Asked in a Dream For A Poem about the Master

Of Barry Spacks (1931–2014).

In Red Pine's Commentary on *the Heart Sutra*

Red Pine (2004) pg 79.

Lines 2–3: Personal communication Gary Snyder.

Line 11: Master Chef Kinya Aota encouraging his curry rice, Bei, Japan.

Jane Hirshfield's Comment During an Interview

The Beauty Jane Hirshfield (2015) pg 38.

Line 3: Jane Hirshfield Interview.

Lines 6 & 8: Personal correspondence.

At a Confluence of Conze Porete Hirshfield and Po Chü-i

Edward Conze in Red Pine (2004) pg 79.

Marguerite Porete in Anne Carson *Decreation* (2005) "Decreation—How Women Like Sappho, Marguerite Porete and Simone Weil Tell God" pgs 163–166.

Jane Hirshfield from *Come, Thief* (2011) "The Supple Deer" pg 87.

Po Chü-i in Hinton (2002) "The North Window: Bamboo and Rock" pg 177.

Li Po Answers a Question about Shame

Lines 9–10: Hinton (1996) "Listening to a Monk's Ch'in Depths" pg 73.

In the Economy of Nature Hearing Joy Harjo

Harjo (2015) pg 126.

See also *The Survivor: An Anatomy Of Life In The Death Camps* (1976) Terrence Des Pres "Life In Death"—*'gift morality' and a will toward communion are constitutive elements of humaness. In extremity, behavior of this kind emerges without plan or instruction, simply as the means to life* pgs 98–147.

Line 4: Harjo (2015) pg 6.

Learning That Ticks Are Born with Six Legs

Red Pine (2004) lines 21–23 pgs 2–3.

See also *Tomas Tranströmer: the great enigma* (2006) Robin Fulton, Translator "Vermeer" *And the wall is part of yourself . . . except for small children. No walls for them.* pgs 190–191.

Captured by W.S. Merwin's Poem *Still* and Its Last Line

Merwin (2014) "Still" pg 53.

William enclosed a drawing of his beloved Coquette's shoe in a letter with her hoofprints walking off beyond the edge of the page.

Line 4: Mantra of *The Heart of the Prajnaparamita Sutra*—Dan Gerber Translation.

Assassination School and Your Wise Blood Question So Young Federico

Arvio (2017) "Trees" pg 17.

Line 6: *Federico García Lorca Collected Poems* (2002) C. Maurer, Editor, "New Heart" *Like a snake, my heart / has shed its skin. / I hold it there in my hands, / full of honey and wounds.* pg 7.

Dante and the Last Candle

Selected Translations W.S. Merwin (2013) "Canto XXVI" *Inferno* pg 317.

Third Chapter Epigraph

Jaime de Angulo (2006) "The Fool behind the Wall" pg 95.

ii

Line 5: *Inanna* Diane Wolkstein & Samuel Noah Kramer (1983) pgs xvi–xvii.

iii

Line 2: *Bible* KJV Matthew 5:8 *Blessed are the pure in heart: for they shall see God.*

Lines 7–8: Hinton (2002) "On Yellow-Crane Tower, Farewell to Meng Hao-jan Who's Leaving for Yang-chou" pg 78.

Line 17: Second Vatican Council 1962–1965 John XXIII & Paul VI "Dogmatic Constitution on Divine Revelation": *(despite bodily death) God called man and still calls him to an eternal imperishable communion of his whole nature with the divine Life*—echoes of the formal classical Pagan education with *the mysteries* initiations of Hilary (310–367 c.e.) later Bishop of Poitiers and Sainthood.

iv

Lines 7–8: Maurer (2002) "Corazon nuevo" pgs 7–8 for the Spanish original—Caleb Beissert translation.

v

Lines 2–4: *Musō Soseki Poems and Sermons* (1989) W.S. Merwin & Sōiku Shigamatsu, Translators pg. 66.

vi

Line 4: Hinton (2008) "Cloud" pg 304.

Lines 5–6: Stephen Hawking lecture UCSB 1987 with my son Amos when he was twelve—"Black Holes, Baby Universes, and Time."

vii

Lines 5–6: Carson (2002) "168C" pg 345.

Lines 10–13: First words said to me by Ekaterina Anna Oxana Galiyeva (1969–2014). See also *The Beatitudes of Ekaterina* (2017) *Nectars of your fragments deepen the wine* pg 79; *Starlight in the dead eye of a poor gold-finch, / tendrils of Milky Way unfurl in a wheeling dot—do your hips turn its turning at that tango dance hall / on the other side of the Swan, Katya?* pg 69.

x

Line 1: Hinton (2008) T'ao Ch'ien "Drinking Wine" *3 & 5 Way's been ruins a thousand years / whenever I start / to explain it, I forget words altogether* pg 117.

Line 6: Carson (2005) *Socrates also puts a fair amount of faith in his own poetic imagination—his power to turn nothing into something* pg 39.

Acknowledgments

I am grateful to the editors and publishers who selected these poems some of them in versions since revised. Brief title versions employed below.

Alabama Literary Review 2019
—Crawling from Home in My Diaper at Ten Months
—A Rage Too Complicated Sought Mei Yao-Ch'en
—105 Degrees Already This Morning
—Old Friends Say They Would Stop and Visit
—After I Found My Father's Body
—Clouds Mixed with the Smoke
—A Fifty Dollar Bill Flutters out of a Book
—Yang Wan'li's Line and the Possible
—To the Woman Who Made a Wide Detour to Avoid Me
—Idling on the Porch with Tu Fu Pondering
—I Turn to Grandmother's Things for Succor
—Mad Thug President Seeks to Roll Back

California Quarterly Spring 2020
—x, xi, xii, xiii, xiv

Live Encounters December 2018
—When I Steered My Father
—Apart from Righteous Fury at the Neo-Nazis
—Li Po Scolded by Blossoms You Let Your Grief Go
—Taxonomy of a Prayer
—Falling into a Metaphysical Abyss

Live Encounters December 2019
—Admiring Ridgelines Above the Valley
—I Grasp the Horns of the Sublime
—in the Economy of Nature Hearing Joy Harjo
—i, iii, v, vi

Sleet Magazine Fall-Winter 2018–2019
—After Fifty Years Return to the Beans
—Unfurling the Rivers and Mountains Scroll
—Although Forbidden I Played a Few Chords
—My Father Taught Me Many Strange Things
—Wordless Sudden Awakening upon Finding
—On W.S. Merwin's *Elegy for a Walnut Tree*
—Startled by the Mind in Merwin's Couplet
—Memory and the Paradoxes of Time
—Asked in a Dream for a Poem About the Master
—If This the Last Thing I Say

All gratitude Stancey Hancock for living every version and steadfast friends Nancy Gifford and Steven Braff. Thank you Ron Colone and the Arts Advocacy Foundation. All love my brother poets Josh Gaines and Caleb Beissert, and sister writer Sophfronia Scott who inspires toward spiritual grace. Applause my brother Mark Russell Jones creator of the cover art—fellow traveler shoulder to shoulder toward our *Wild Church* and beyond. As always a special thank you to Dan Gerber who transcends as friend, poet, and close reader. To Mariaelena Susana Camareña and Kristen Goforth. Salud Bobby Moy who has translated wine into poetry at his *Chiron* cellars with Tiana and Cayo Juni Moy. Timeless abrazos y besos Edmund Kara, Eduardo Tirella, Phyllis (Gypsy) Coates, Howard Press, Jane Hirshfield, W.S. Merwin, and spiritual father— Jaime de Angulo. Many poets and translators virtually formed my being making the conversations of these poems natural expressions of that life's way—and I hope received as gratitude and homage—particularly W.S. Merwin, Jane Hirshfield, David Hinton, Red Pine, Jaime de Angulo, Anne Carson, Yun Wang, Sam Hamill, Sarah Arvio, Joy Harjo, Robin Fulton, Patrick Donnelly, Carolyn Forché, Marsha de la O, Jaime Sabines, Zbigniew Herbert, Charles Simic, Gary Snyder, Caleb Beissert, and the Chinese masters throughout the ages. Thank you.

About the Author

Richard Jarrette is author of *Beso the Donkey* (Michigan State University Press, 2010) Gold Medal Poetry Midwest Independent Publishers Association 2011, *A Hundred Million Years of Nectar Dances* (Green Writers Press, 2015), *The Beatitudes of Ekaterina* (Green Writers Press 2017), and *The Pond* (Green Writers Press, 2019). Jarrette's books received advance praise from W.S. Merwin, Joseph Stroud, Jane Hirshfield, and Sam Hamill. After formative years in the Southern Appalachian Highlands of North Carolina he is considered a regional Appalachian writer as well as Central California Coast where he lives semi-reclusively after a forty-five year career as a psychotherapist.

Photograph of the author by Mark Russell Jones.
Used by permission.

Free Verse Editions

Edited by Jon Thompson

13 ways of happily by Emily Carr
& in Open, Marvel by Felicia Zamora
Alias by Eric Pankey
Ariadne, A Series by Martha Ronk
At Your Feet (A Teus Pés) by Ana Cristina César, edited by Katrina Dodson, trans. by Brenda Hillman and Helen Hillman
Bari's Love Song by Kang Eun-Gyo, translated by Chung Eun-Gwi
Between the Twilight and the Sky by Jennie Neighbors
Blood Orbits by Ger Killeen
The Bodies by Christopher Sindt
The Book of Isaac by Aidan Semmens
The Calling by Bruce Bond
Canticle of the Night Path by Jennifer Atkinson
Child in the Road by Cindy Savett
Civil Twilight by Giles Goodland
Condominium of the Flesh by Valerio Magrelli, trans. by Clarissa Botsford
Contrapuntal by Christopher Kondrich
Country Album by James Capozzi
Cry Baby Mystic by Daniel Tiffany
The Curiosities by Brittany Perham
Current by Lisa Fishman
Day In, Day Out by Simon Smith
Dear Reader by Bruce Bond
Dismantling the Angel by Eric Pankey
Divination Machine by F. Daniel Rzicznek
Elsewhere, That Small by Monica Berlin
Empire by Tracy Zeman
Erros by Morgan Lucas Schuldt
Fifteen Seconds without Sorrow by Shim Bo-Seon, trans. by Chung Eun-Gwi and Brother Anthony of Taizé
The Forever Notes by Ethel Rackin
The Flying House by Dawn-Michelle Baude
Ghost Letters by Baba Badji
Go On by Ethel Rackin
Here City by Rick Snyder
Instances: Selected Poems by Jeongrye Choi, trans. by Brenda Hillman, Wayne de Fremery, & Jeongrye Choi
Last Morning by Simon Smith